Walking in
Oneness

Walking in
Oneness

Taking the Father by the hand

"May they be One, as we are One …"
(John 17: 22)

Christine Nelson

authorHOUSE®

AuthorHouse™
1663 Liberty Drive
Bloomington, IN 47403
www.authorhouse.com
Phone: 1-800-839-8640

Published by AuthorHouse   05/18/2012

ISBN: 978-1-4685-0498-9 (sc)
ISBN: 978-1-4685-7767-9 (e)

Contents

Acknowledgement

To my other half, my best friend, my greatest supporter, my lover, my wonderful husband, Omowale, who has always encouraged me in all my endeavours. I love you. Thank you for always believing in me and encouraging me to live out my dreams.

To my children Kobi and Kristian, my blessings from above. Thank you, Kobi, for always encouraging me and making me feel invincible. Bless you, my sweet. You are my prince.

Kristian, though you were only five months old when I started this journey, you have been such a sweetie—sleeping during the first half of the night and affording me the time to write. Thank you, my darling. You are my sunshine.

To my very supportive father, who has been a great source of encouragement and inspiration. Thank you for trusting me and being resourceful by sourcing publishers for this book. May God bless your beautiful heart. I love you.

To my spiritual mother and friend, Joanne Naughton, who has read, helped me to edit, and given me specific input as to how to improve my writing. Your love, support, and input have been invaluable.

To my cell leader, friend, and big sister, Mary Ewuosho, who has always been a great source of encouragement and inspiration. It was in fact a message taught by Mary about the prayer of Jesus in John 17 that prompted me to study Jesus' prayer in detail. Thank you for always loving me for who I am and nurturing me accordingly.

To my dear friend Abimbola Oguntunde, who has been a great source of encouragement. She also thoroughly read and edited this book. I am so grateful for all your input and help.

To my dear friend Joanne Johnson, who has been an angel sent by God to support me with some invaluable editorial insights. Thank you, my angel. God bless you for your labour of love.

To my valued friend Kay, for reading through and editing—despite having four children to take care of.

To my cell members Nadine, Mina, and Rachel, who were the first to make it known to me that I could write a book. They announced after one lesson I taught that the message should be a book. I am eternally grateful to all of you for being such an encouragement.

Thank you to Defini Photography for breathing life into an idea to produce the most magnificent book cover. Genius!

Dedication

I would like to dedicate this book to my Daddy in heaven. This book is a real testimony to how, by walking in oneness with God, anything can be made possible.

After I had my second child I confided in the Lord that I was bored. I needed something else to do while I was being a mummy. I then reminded Him of a time when I thought He was prompting me to write a book. I asked Him about it and suddenly in a rush my Daddy, our Father, gave me a series of books on oneness.

As days went by, when I was driving, cooking, or tidying the house, the Lord would talk to me about different chapters of this book, and I took notes. As the Lord gave me divine revelations and I practised these very principles, the book became more of a reality.

This book is a testimony to how, when you value God's approval above man's, He can do anything with you, through you, and in you so that you can be a blessing to others. I am so grateful to God, because to write a book was only a dream, but God has made it a reality. Though I compiled this book, I strongly believe this book was birthed by the power of the Holy Spirit. To God be the glory!

The Journey

This book is made up of ten chapters. I believe each chapter is made up of ten key principles that can ignite the oneness Jesus prayed about. By the power of the Holy Spirit, when these principles are applied, they will revolutionize your relationship with God.

Each chapter summarises the key points, which are bulleted. This is done in order to assist you, the reader, to apply the principles in a practical way. At the end of each chapter there is a prayer which can be used as a guide to pray. All the prayers are written in the first person to make them easier to use or adapt.

Each chapter is written independently of the others. Therefore, it is not critical that you read in chapter order. Furthermore, you can boost your study by reading according to your need or the prompting of the Holy Spirit. However, I must add that an understanding of all the chapters is crucial to grasp the power of oneness in your relationship with God.

If you desire to study the notion of oneness further, there are some biblical references that can enhance your study. I pray that as you go on this amazing journey of exploring Jesus' prayer of oneness, your life will never be the same again.

To God be the glory!

Foreword

Christine has a fresh, unspoiled voice in song and in writing. She loves Christ with all her heart and has a desire that others should come to know His love too. She also sees the truth in God's word and wants to give others a true picture of what it means to be in Christ.

Christine has taken scriptural truth and translated it into such practical application that there will be no excuse for not grasping the valuable insight she shares. Christine also knows how important it is that each person has a clear knowledge of the love of Christ and who they are in Christ, and that is what oneness is all about. In these pages she reveals how the Lord Jesus Christ was one with his Father and why we should also be one with the Lord.

For those seeking greater intimacy with the Lord, I know this book will be a great blessing.

Be blessed as you read.

Mary Ewuosho
Minister of the Word
Harvest Church

Introduction

On September 11 2001 there was a terrorist attack on the United States of America. Some of the passengers who were on those planes had the chance to phone their loved ones. They knew that the plane would crash into a building in a matter of minutes. They were aware that they did not have time to talk about the mundane things in life. They were precise, ensuring that what they said was of paramount importance. Recognizing the importance of these last communications, their loved ones would endeavour to fulfil whatever request was made.

Similarly, Jesus knew when His time on earth was drawing to a close. He was aware that He was about to undergo the most agonizing of deaths. Before this ordeal, He took time to bid His disciples goodbye, talking to them about many important things. However, the very last significant thing He did was to offer up prayers for His disciples (recorded in John 17) that detailed what was in His heart at that time. We can conclude that everything in that prayer was of paramount importance to Him and to us, His modern-day disciples. We must therefore peruse this famous prayer of Jesus in order to fulfil that which He desired most for us. One of the key concerns of His was *oneness.*

Throughout Jesus' prayer He highlights the need for us to be one, like He and the Father were one, as seen in John 17: 22.

Christine Nelson

". . . May they be one as we are one . . ."

What does oneness or to be one mean? It can be described as complete unbroken unity between two or more persons. In the context of Jesus' prayer for us as Christians, oneness refers specifically to our relationship with God.

Oneness is conforming yourself to the nature of God.

> *Strip yourselves of your former nature which characterized your previous manner of life. (Ephesians 4: 22)*

Oneness is flowing in the mind-set of God.

> *And be constantly renewed in the spirit of your mind (having a fresh mental and spiritual attitude). (Ephesians 4: 23)*

Oneness is synchronizing heaven's agenda with earth's.

> *. . . the Son can do nothing by Himself. He does only what He sees the Father doing. (John 5: 19-20)*

Oneness is living out the very image we were created in.

> *. . . and have put on the new self who is being renewed to a true knowledge according to the image of the One who created him. (Colossians 3: 10)*

Oneness is being whole—all that you can be.

> *For in Christ lives all the fullness of God in a human body. So you also are complete through your union with Christ. (Colossians 2: 9-10)*

Oneness is walking with our Creator hand in hand.

> *Can two people walk together without agreeing on the direction? (Amos 3: 3)*

Oneness is the fuel that makes the impossible possible.

> *. . . If as one people speaking the same language they have begun to do this, then nothing they plan to do will be impossible for them. (Genesis 11: 6)*

Oneness is divinely connecting with the power of God.

> *We now have this light shining in our hearts, but we ourselves are like fragile clay jars containing this great treasure. This makes it clear that our great power is from God, not from ourselves. (2 Corinthians 4: 7)*

One might ask, what is the significance of this oneness and why is it so important?

I believe that if we were to live our lives focused on being one with Jesus, we would have an unbroken fellowship with God, because in Romans 6: 10 it reads:

> *For by the death He died, He died to sin (ending His relation to it) once for all; and the life that He lives, He is living to God in (unbroken fellowship with Him).*

So you see, to live a life unto God is to have an unbroken fellowship with God. No longer would it be my way, but God's way instead. We would be allowing Jesus to live through us, continuously aligning our mind, our will, and our emotions to that of Christ's. Inevitably, by walking in oneness we would be defeating Satan and walking in a greater anointing. Ultimately, we would be fulfilling our God-given call, and His dreams for our lives would become a reality.

When looking at oneness, you must also consider its opposite, which is to be divided, to be disunited, or to be scattered. If Jesus talked so much about oneness (drawing all men to Himself), then division must be detestable before God.

In reality the world in which we live often presents us with situations that seek to divide and cause disunity among us. In his book *Oneness in the Mingled Spirit*, Witness Lee states that "by being divided or scattered, man has become useless in the hands of God." Therefore, by being one with Christ, we become useful in the hands of God.

Without the manifestation of this oneness, the world will not be able to recognize Jesus as the Son of God. This emphasizes the need to grasp and pursue the oneness of Christ. By doing this, people will recognize Christ in us. Also, those who are lost will be won for Jesus, and to God be the glory.

Prayer

Lord, as I embark on this journey to understand the power of walking in oneness with You, I pray that You will bring divine revelation. Lord, as I read and pray, give me the grace to put into practise what You, O God, are saying to me personally. I thank You, because I know that with every revelation my mind will be renewed and I will be changed from glory to glory. I give You thanks, O God, for what You are doing now even as You prepare my heart and for what You will do as I read these pages. I thank You in advance, because I know my relationship with You will never be the same again. In Jesus' Name, Amen!

Chapter 1

Prayer of Oneness

My prayer is not for the world but for those you have given me, because they belong to you; and you have given back to me, so they are my glory! Now I am departing from the world; I am leaving them behind and coming to you. Holy Father, keep them and care for them—all those you have given me. So that they will be united just as we are. During my time here, I have kept them safe. I guarded them so that no one was lost except the one headed for destruction as the scriptures foretold and now I am coming. I have told them many things while I was with them so they would be filled with my joy. I have given them your word and the world hates them because they do not belong to the world, just as I do not. I'm not asking you to take them because they do not belong to the world but to keep them safe from the evil one. They are not part of the world any more than I am. Make them pure and holy by teaching them words of truth. As you sent me into the world I am sending them into the world. I give myself entirely so they also might be entirely yours. I am praying not only for those disciples but also for all who will ever believe in me because of their testimony. My prayer for all of them is that they

1

will be one just as You and I are one, Father—that just as you are in me I am in you so they will be in us, and the world will believe you sent me. I have given them the glory you have given me so that they may be one as We are one—I in them and You in Me, all being perfected into one. Then the world will know that you sent me and will understand that you love me. Father, I want these whom you've given me to be with me, so they can see my glory. You gave me the glory because you loved me even before the world began!

O righteous Father, the world doesn't know but I do, and these disciples know you sent me. And I have revealed you to them and will keep on revealing you. I will do this that your love for me may be in them and I in them. (John 17: 9-26)

> Prayer begins in heaven in the heart of God.

Throughout this prayer there is a recurring theme of being one. This prayer encapsulates so magnificently what was in the heart of God at that time. We know this because Jesus said:

. . . the Son can do nothing by Himself. He does only what He sees the Father doing. Whatever the Father does, the Son also does. For the Father loves the Son and shows Him everything He is doing. (John 5: 19-20)

Jesus prayed the very heart of God, synchronizing heaven and earth. You see, prayer begins in heaven in the heart of God. Then the Lord prompts us by the Holy Spirit on earth. As we pray, our prayer returns to heaven. This is how Jesus taught us to pray in Luke 11: 2 "Your will be done on earth as it is in heaven." This principle highlights that God wants heaven to partner with us on earth, but this only happens when we pray God's will. For our prayers to be effective, they must begin in heaven and end in heaven. This cycle is crucial for us to engage in oneness of prayer so as to walk hand in hand with the Lord.

The Cycle of Prayer

What are the benefits of praying as one?

First, we need to ask ourselves what prayer is. Prayer is a two-way communication between us and God. Praying in oneness can be described as praying in agreement with God Himself. To agree with what God has said in His word (the Bible), or what you are being prompted to pray by His Spirit. In effect, to pray as one is to pray the very will and desire of God.

Throughout the Bible there are examples of praying according to the will of God. It was the prayer of Simeon and

Anna in Luke 2: 25, 36-38 that brought forth the birth of Jesus. Interestingly, although the Holy Spirit was promised by Jesus, it was the prayers of the one hundred and twenty disciples in the upper room that caused the Holy Spirit to descend in Acts 2. You see, God had promised, but it was the prayer of the saints that synchronized heaven with earth.

In Genesis 11: 31 Abraham's father Terah was told by God to go to the Land of Canaan, but instead Terah settled and died in Haran. I believe that after Terah died Abraham was at a crossroads in his life. He asked God for an answer as to what his next move should be. God told Abraham (then called Abram):

> *Leave your country, your relatives and your father's house, and go to the land that I will show you. (Genesis 12: 1)*

Heaven synchronizes with earth when we pray the promises of God.

Here it is. God has asked Abraham to leave all he knows and go to an unspecified land. I am almost sure that even as Abraham packed with the intention of leaving his family and not being able to say where he was going, he must have had second thoughts about his decision to leave. Here, Abraham and God are having a conversation where, in prayer, God instructs Abraham. Yet because Abraham followed the voice of God, trusting in His Word, he became the father of many nations. Today billions of people are blessed through Abraham's obedience and faith in God, because as God promised Abraham, all the blessings he received are now ours in Christ.

We also see an example of this oneness of prayer when we pray as a church in one accord.

> *"They lifted their voices together as one, united in mind to God and said, O Sovereign Lord, You are He who made the heaven and the earth and the sea and everything that is in them . . . " (Acts 4: 24)*

This prayer resulted in them being divinely enabled to stand up for the gospel despite opposition. Again, in Acts 12: 5-10, the church knew of Peter's impending fate and of the enemy's plan to destroy God's servant. They fervently prayed, taking hold of God and asking for Peter's release. They were still praying through the night, when the iron gates opened and freed Peter from the prison bars that held him captive. Evidently, praying as one has the potential to make the impossible possible.

The Lord revealed to me the significance of this oneness in prayer through a personal experience. I was pregnant with my second child and was reading a book which greatly emphasized supernatural childbirth. I prayed on *Praying as one makes the impossible possible.* and off about having a painless childbirth. I described my prayer as on/off because as the impending date drew closer, I felt the pressure to pray even more about having a painless birth. As you know, it takes time to renew one's mind. I had one child before without the knowledge of supernatural childbirth, and I assure you it was not painless. In fact, that experience only made me more desperate for this birth to be supernaturally pain-free.

As I prayed, I kept feeling as though my prayers were empty and meaningless, and instead I felt an urgency to pray against the enemy's plan for the birth to result in caesarean section.

The day to give birth came. Everything was going well until it was time to push. Although I was pushing with all my might for over two hours, my baby was nowhere in sight! Before long, I was told they would assist me to deliver with the ventouse (a vacuum device used to assist with the delivery of a baby), and if this was unsuccessful, they would use the forceps (which are placed on either side of the baby's head so the doctor can pull the baby out as the mother pushes). Moreover, if these methods both proved futile, they would do a C-section.

Before I could make sense of what was being said, I was being wheeled into the theatre. A feeling of fear and horror gripped me. My tears quickly welled up and moistened my eyes. I stubbornly fought back my tears. I was pleading with my birth partner to pray! As I left the room, I began to talk to the Lord. I told Him that I didn't want an operation but that if the procedure became life-threatening to my baby or to myself, then He was to do whatever needed to be done. I felt such peace when I prayed. I surrendered my fears as much as I could at the time and tried to relax.

In the end I gave birth without needing any major medical intervention. I was so grateful to God for His grace towards me and our baby. I was so amazed when I considered the entire sequence of events and how God intervened just in time. I believed that Satan had planned for me to have a C-section with the intention to steal and destroy, but because I obeyed the prompting of God to pray against having a major operation, the enemy's plan was aborted. In this situation I was praying to God for supernatural childbirth manifested in a pain-free delivery. However, as I prayed, the Holy Spirit was leading me to pray against a surgical intervention.

To pray according to the will of God and His promptings is to walk in oneness with Him. This adds remarkable power to our prayers. When heaven and earth are in agreement, our prayers are propelled supernaturally. It is no longer a matter of whether our prayers will be answered or not, because when our prayers are led by the Spirit of God, they will be effective. Our prayers will no longer be self-centred or self-serving but directed by the Spirit of God.

> *When heaven and earth are in agreement, our prayers are propelled supernaturally.*

How do we know if we are praying in oneness with God? We need to ask ourselves questions like:

- Am I being sensitive to the spirit of God?
- Am I praying when prompted?
- Am I praying my agenda or God's agenda?
- Am I walking in presumption or faith?
- Am I praying according to the word of God?

Prayer

Father in heaven, thank You that heaven can synchronize with earth as I obey your promptings to pray. Lord, I thank

Christine Nelson

You for every promise and prophetic word You have given me as a prayer point. Father, I thank You, for no longer will I pray aimlessly. I will pray with power and effectiveness. All that seems impossible will become possible because I pray in oneness with You. I thank You for the divine results because of this oneness. Father, open my eyes so that like Jesus I will only do and say what You would do in heaven. I thank You for the grace to operate in this mind-set. In Jesus' name, Amen!

Chapter 2

Jesus, Our Example

One of the most awesome characteristics of Jesus is that He never asks us to do anything He has not done Himself. Jesus repeatedly spoke with great emphasis on the oneness He shared with the Father. In the latter part of John 17:2 Jesus prayed, "Father, the hour has come; glorify Thy Son, that the Son may glorify Thee."

Here Jesus implies that as He and the Father are one and as He is glorified, so is the Father. This oneness He refers to can be described as being united or one in the same. Paul wrote in Colossians 1: 15 that Jesus is the exact representation of God the Father. I would like to use this analogy to explain further.

God the Father is like the sun. He brings light into our lives; He sustains us; He is all-powerful. Jesus on the other hand is like the rays of the sun. He is God, but we are better able to relate to Him because of His humanity. The actual sun is connected to its rays as one. If you see the sun, you will feel the rays, and vice versa. In the same way, God and the Son are one. All the fullness of the Father dwells in the

Son (Colossians 1: 19 and 2: 9) and is expressed through the Son (John 1: 18).

In John 10: 30 Jesus spoke of this oneness. In verse 30 the word for "one" in the Greek is *hen,* which does not mean one person but one in essence, power, and quality. Even though previously in John 10:29, Jesus said, "My Father who has given them to me, is greater than all; and no one is able to snatch them out of the Father's hand," when reading both verses 29 and 30, it is possible to interpret this as Jesus contradicting himself. "But what He meant was that to snatch His disciples out of His hand would be to snatch them out of His Father's hand, because He and the Father are one in power, design, action, agreement, and essence." (Notes from The New American Standard Bible Key Word Study Bible Hebrew-Greek pg.1572).

Jesus refers to the oneness He has with the father in verse 11, where He prays "that they may be one as We are one." From these examples we see that Jesus obviously understood the significance of His oneness with God the Father. He both prayed it and lived it. In the lead-up to His death Jesus endured

> *God the Son and God the Father are one in power, design, action, agreement and essence.*

emotional, physical, and spiritual pain. However, He cried out only once—at the point He experienced separation from God. In Matthew 27: 46 Jesus cries out, "My God, My God, why have you forsaken me?" God the Father, Jesus, and the Holy Spirit had always walked in oneness. This was the first time in history they were being separated, because Jesus had taken on the sins of the world and the Father could not associate with sin. This being heart-wrenching for Jesus, He cried out again in Matthew 27, and the Bible records that it was only then that Jesus gave up His spirit. In fact, we could deduce that this oneness was so important to Jesus that when the oneness shared between the Triune God had been broken, He no longer felt the need to fight His impending death. He gave up His Spirit willingly. This only highlights that Jesus lived for and was complete in this oneness with the Father. Without this oneness, life is empty and meaningless.

What is the significance of Jesus' oneness with the Father?

Although Jesus knew of His equality with God, in Philippians 2: 6 the scripture says that *"He did not regard equality with God a thing to be grasped."* Instead He submitted to God the Father by relying on Him in all things. In other words, though Jesus knew that He was God, He did nothing in His power but completely surrendered to the authority of God the Father and walked with God as one. In the same way that Jesus is an expression of the Father, God wants us to be an expression of Jesus. For this to be a reality, we like Jesus, must submit or align ourselves with the will of God. If we refrain from following the Father's lead, we run the risk of causing ourselves grief and frustration because we cannot accomplish God's best in our own strength. Philippians 4:19 says that "we can do all things through Christ who gives us strength." The opposite of this scripture is also true: it could read "We can't do anything without the strength of Christ!" I believe this is why Jesus prayed so fervently for us to be one as He is one with the Father. You see, Jesus put aside His agenda,

> *To walk as Jesus did, is to become one in the same sense that Jesus and the Father are one.*

His position, and His titles to pursue the Father's. For us to be a true expression of Jesus, we must do the same.

In 1 John 2, the Apostle John wrote that we should walk as Jesus did. So how can we walk like Jesus? In John 17: 11 and 21-22, Jesus prayed for His disciples to become one (*hen*) in the same sense that He and the Father are one. He was certainly not implying that we become one person but that His desires become ours, His ways become ours, or His way of thinking become ours—ultimately, that we should walk in His divine will and purpose.

When I was seeking God's will about whether I was to do my Master's in Education, I was three months pregnant with my second child and my marriage was struggling. Although I was seeking God, it was difficult to align my will with His, I knew that He wanted me to wait. I was eager to proceed with my studies because of my age and the fact that I wanted to finish my studies so that my children would benefit from them. Even though my reasoning sounded sensible, God wanted me to wait! Though I was praying about it, I had not surrendered my will, my age, or my desires. So when I got a lot of attention from lecturers who were trying to recruit me to different Master's courses, I was flattered and became less prayerful, and I made a decision contrary to my initial instinct. The consequences of my disobedience resulted in me having a still birth twenty-eight weeks into the pregnancy. More visible holes were highlighted in my marriage, and I went through one of the most difficult times of my life. I am not saying God was responsible for what I went through, but had I been obedient, the outcome could have been different. This example highlights how crucial it is that we align our will, emotions, and thoughts with the

Lord's. We must trust in His wisdom and stand confident in the knowledge that He knows the beginning from the end. It could save us so much pain and adversity.

In Philippians 2 Paul describes the attitude of Jesus that enabled Him to walk in this oneness.

- We must have the mind of Christ, i.e., think like Christ. (v. 5)
- We must forget about our rights, our position, and making a name for ourselves, our self-importance or self-exaltation. (v. 6)
- We must emphasize character (how God sees us) rather than reputation (how people see us). (v. 7)
- We must be obedient to the Spirit of God, not to the soul (mind, will, and emotions). (v. 8)

Prayer

Father, I thank You for Jesus and His example to be one with You and the Holy Spirit. Thank You that Your agenda was His. May it also be mine. Your dream and mission for His life were His dream and mission. May I be one with your dream and mission for my life. I receive grace to set aside my mind-set, my rights, position, self-importance, and self-exaltation. I receive grace to imitate the humility of Jesus and the obedient spirit that He displayed. O Lord, when I am no longer walking with You as One, may I, like Jesus, become one with You so that when sin separates me from our close relationship, my heart is quick to repent to walk in oneness with You. May You exalt the Christ in me so the world may know that He is Lord. In Jesus' name Amen.

Chapter 3

Followers that Follow

Jesus chose to reproduce his ministry in his followers. He did this because of his conviction that we are one with Him. Jesus' prayer in John 17: 10 describes the oneness that his followers at the time and those to come would share with Him.

In verse 10 Jesus prayed, *"And all things that are Mine are Yours, and Yours are Mine; and I have been glorified in them."*

In verses 14 and 16 He again repeatedly declares *"They are not of the world, even as I am not of the world."*

Again describing this oneness, whatever He is not, the same is true of us (His followers). Consequently, the opposite is true: whatever He is, so are we; the latter part of 1 John 4:17 emphasizes the same principle. Furthermore, verse 10 reiterates another fact, that whatever is Jesus' is also yours and mine. The following table illustrates this fact.

From the Father to the Son to His children

Father	The Son	Children
The Father judges. John 8: 16	The Son judges. John 8: 16	Children judge. 1 Corinthians 6: 1-5
God is light. 1 John 1: 5	I am the light of the world. John 8: 12, John 12: 46	Children live in the light of God's presence. Matthew 5: 14, 1 John 1: 7
The Father teaches. John 8: 28	The Son teaches. John 8: 28	Children teach. Acts 5: 42, 1 Timothy 3: 2 1 Timothy 4: 11
The Father gave His Son. 1 John 3: 16	The Son gave His life. John 10: 11	Children lay down their lives for one another. 1 John 3: 16
The Father is perfect. Matthew 5: 48	The Son is perfect. Matthew 5: 48	Children are made perfect in their weaknesses. 2 Corinthians 12: 9, Colossians 3: 10

> *God wants us to bear the image of Christ*

From this table, you can see that there is a clear pattern of the Father's actions, Jesus' actions, and the actions of his children. This illustrates the unity and oneness shared between God the Father, Jesus, and his children through the power of the Holy Spirit. Jesus is the image of God in human form. God simply wants his people to bear his image.

The majority of Jesus' prayer was praying for us, his disciples. Our Lord knew that the success of his ministry when He ascended to heaven was dependent on the twelve He had trained, and those to come. In John 17:11-26, Jesus prays for seven attributes for his disciples.

- our faith to be sustained (v. 11-12)
- our joy to be fulfilled (v. 13)
- our protection from the enemy (v. 14, 15)
- our sanctification (v. 16-17)
- our fruitfulness (v. 18-20)
- our oneness with God and fellow man (v. 21-23)
- our love (v. 24-26)

The apostle Paul, I believe, was an outstanding example of being one with Christ. Paul told the church in Corinth *"that the thing that has made him so upset is that He cares about them so much. It is the passion of God burning inside him."* (2 Corinthians 11: 2, Message translation).

> *God's agenda and passion was Paul's. May it be ours.*

God's agenda and passion was Paul's. I sometimes wonder how it was that Paul was able to write the majority of the

New Testament and plant so many churches despite the imprisonments and hardships that he endured. I believe Paul was focused on accomplishing whatever the Lord had assigned him. Therefore, he did not allow his circumstances to distract him from seeing his assignment through to completion. I believe Paul understood the importance of being one with Christ, so he pursued and hungered for it at all times.

In fact, Paul said:

> *Everything else is worthless when compared with the priceless gain of knowing Christ my Lord. I have discarded everything else counting it all garbage, so I may have Christ and become one with Him. I no longer count on my goodness or my ability to obey God's law, but I trust Christ and become one with God's law, but I trust Christ to save me, for God's way of making us right with himself depends on faith. As a result, I can really know Christ and experience the mighty power that raised him from the dead. I can learn what it means to suffer with him, sharing in his death, so that, somehow, I can experience the resurrection from the dead! (Philippians 3: 8-10, New Living Translation)*

Our effort to walk in righteousness is futile when compared to our need to be one with Christ.

Paul realised that it was not by his might or his power that he would be able to obey God's commandments. He knew his own efforts to be righteous were futile when compared to his need to be one with Christ. To become holy is a choice we must make as Christians. However, we cannot become holy on our own. I believe Paul realised that his efforts to follow the law were stopping him from being one with Christ. Instead, he put aside all he gained or achieved from his own righteousness and trusted Christ by becoming one with God's law. He recognized that he was saved by faith in Christ, and so he relied on his faith in Christ to help him walk in oneness thus holiness. Alternatively, he put all his efforts into truly knowing Christ so as to walk in oneness with Him.

Before I became a Christian I was a compulsive liar. I hated lying because I knew that as a result of my lies people would not trust me. At the beginning of everyday I would pray to the Lord, "Help me to be truthful today." As I went through the day, I found myself lying even about things I had no need to lie about. You see, I was trying to use my will to stop lying. My mind-set of being "sin-conscious" only made me sin even more. Even when I became a Christian, it took me years to realise that I could not change myself. Moreover, my will is not powerful enough to help me to stay on the straight and narrow path. This lack of understanding made me more and more frustrated in Christ, rather than finding my rest in Him. Instead I found that if I focused more on who I had become in Christ, I would be allowing Christ to work through me. This really helped me to walk more in God's truth, because the more you know Christ, the more you know who you are in Him.

> *To know Christ is to know who you are in Him*

Paul desired to know Jesus so personally that he wanted to know Him in his power, in his suffering, and in his death. What does it mean to know Christ in his suffering, death, and power? I think Paul was convicted by 1 John 4: 17b,

19

where it says, "As Jesus is so are we in this world." Paul knew that if he were to be one with Christ, he had to die to himself like Jesus did. Thus when faced with death, he would portray the same selflessness and focus as Jesus did. Paul had to go through hardships like Christ and then rise in the power of Christ, not himself. For Paul or any of us to become like Christ in this way, we must truly become imitators of Christ.

Power

The question is, "Whose power are you walking in?" As Christians we have a "power of attorney". This is the promise of unlimited power that Jesus willingly gives us. In John 14: 12 Jesus promised that anyone who believes will do same and even greater works than He did. This power is ours not because of who we are but because of who lives in us.

Suffering and Death

> *To live out the desires and will of God is to walk in oneness.*

Will we suffer and die as Christians? Yes, because as Jesus is, so are we in this world. It is in suffering that we are truly being transformed to become more like Christ. This explains the importance of recognizing the reality of us being dead and Christ being alive in us—that is, the need to die to our desires and feelings and will but to live out the desires and will of God.

In 1 Peter 4: 1 it reads, *"Christ suffered for us in the flesh. Arm yourselves likewise with the same mind."* To become like Christ in death is to have the same mind-set as Christ so that the will of God will be accomplished. What was Christ's mind-set?

- To accomplish the will of God for his life.
- To love people more than his life.

Paul's ministry and life are a clear illustration of the fruit that can be born out of living in oneness with Christ Undoubtedly, Paul fulfilled his destiny. Paul told the church in Galatia that God called him to preach and win the Gentiles, and that he did. Furthermore, despite Paul's imprisonments, beatings, and hardships, he never stopped preaching Christ, because he was determined to show the love of God towards the Gentiles. We can see that the seven attributes that Jesus prayed for his disciples were all fulfilled in Paul's life. This was because of his desire and longing to become one with Christ above all else. Are you willing to become one with Christ above all else?

In order for this to be true in our own lives; we must walk in the same mind-set as Christ and:

- Endeavour to know the will of God for our lives and to fulfil it.
- Love others more than ourselves.

Christine Nelson

Prayer

Lord Jesus, thank You that You value me so much that You have made me an heir and partaker of your ministry. Thank You, Father, that You believe in me so much that You made me in your own image, because as Jesus is, so am I in this world. Thank You for praying for these characteristics, which are indicative of me being One with You. May I be expectant of that which You have prayed. It is mine! I endeavour to live out the manifestation of these attributes. I thank You, Lord, for the faith which will sustain me. Thank You for your joy that has fulfilled me. Thank You that I am protected from the enemy, Satan. Thank You that I walk in the truth of Your Word so that I may be sanctified. For those disciples You have given me and for those to come, may I teach them how to be one with You and their fellow man as I walk in peace with all men. Lord, I thank You for your grace to be able to put on your love and walk in it every day. Lord, I thank You that You have a specific plan and purpose for me. Lord, I receive grace to know what my calling is and to do all it takes to fulfil my calling. As Paul ran the race, fixing his eyes on the prize of fulfilling his God-given calling, give me the same focus and tenacity. Lord, like You, I pray I too will consider others above and before myself at all times. In Jesus' name, Amen.

Chapter 4

Emptying Yourself

Did you know that being empty is one of the most powerful places spiritually we can be? Paul writes in 2 Corinthians 12: 9 that Christ's grace (favour) is sufficient for us, for his power is perfected in our weakness. There is something about nothing that moves the hand of God. He loves leading us to empty places where we can lean on nothing except his provision. If we are not experiencing God's presence and provision, could it be that we aren't empty enough? Could we still be distracted and dependent on ourselves?

What does being empty have to do with being one? In Philippians 2: 7 Jesus emptied Himself. The phrase "emptied himself" in Greek is *ekenōse* from the active verb *keno,* which means ploughing or to be silent or to hold one's peace. Jesus voluntarily emptied himself in making his humiliation, suffering, and ultimately his death possible. (Notes from the New American Standard Bible Key Word Study Bible Hebrew-Greek)

In our everyday lives we are given this opportunity to hold our peace. I am often faced with the need to empty myself in my marriage and when training my children. Presently, I am at home full-time, which means that I do most of the housework. There are times when I am so tired and I would love my husband to take the initiative and help me with the dishes or to put the rubbish out. My husband, bless his heart! If you ask him to wash the dishes, he will say, "Okay, honey." The question is never whether he will do it; it is always when he will do it. It might be two days later. Obviously, when I see the dishes unwashed the next day, I am not pleased, and most times I will wash them with resentment.

> *Emptiness makes room for God's power*

One day, while I was washing the dishes and mumbling to myself, I sensed the Lord saying that I was not helping my husband by doing the dishes he said he would do. Then I began to leave them. When I left them I felt so much turmoil, because the kitchen would be a mess. I would become frustrated and nag my husband in the attempt to force his hand.

Eventually I went before God expressing my frustration and my guilt at being a nagging wife. This was because I'd realised that I was losing the battle of wills. The minute I expressed to the Lord my need for his solution rather than my own, I was able to empty myself and hold my peace.

In 1 Corinthians 3: 16 Paul says that he planted the seed, Apollos watered it, and God made it grow. You see, in everything we have a part. God has a part, but so do we. He desires to work in partnership with us. To understand this principle we have to empty ourselves and find out from God what we can do, but equally importantly what we need to leave for Him to do.

Jesus chose to empty himself when He came to earth. He laid down the need for the full recognition of his sovereignty by men. Jesus had freely given up his status, wealth, and position in order for us to gain Him. What are we willing to give up so that we can gain Christ? Today the call is the same—for us to empty ourselves of anything that will stop Christ from being formed in us. It could be self-promotion, offence, position, status, education, talent, knowledge, etc. I believe by emptying ourselves of anything that will hinder us from walking in oneness, we would be able to achieve fellowship with God intimately like never before. The emptier we are, the more it enables God to work through us. The act of emptying yourself releases God to show his power.

In Matthew 26: 36-46 there is a great example of Jesus emptying himself. Here Jesus is in the Garden of Gethsemane praying to the Father because of the heaviness He felt knowing that torture and a brutal death lay ahead of Him.

> *Emptiness helps us to hold our peace.*

The contrast between how Jesus and his disciples responded to the burden of his impending death is captivating. Jesus shared openly with his disciples that He felt "exceedingly sorrowful", and he implored them to stay and watch with Him. In other words, I believe Jesus was saying, "Please watch and pray. I am feeling burdened and vulnerable right now!" In order to watch, you have to have your eyes open. Unfortunately, the disciples' eyes were heavy, and although Jesus had opened his heart to them, it did not motivate them to rise up in prayer to support Him. Instead they fell asleep.

I strongly believe that if the disciples had prayed rather than slept, they would have been empowered to face the other temptations that came thereafter in victory. I believe if they had emptied themselves in prayer by sharing their fears and their anxieties, surely their faith would not have failed them!

Even so, we see the opposite in Jesus. In this time of apprehension Jesus did not close up and isolate himself from his friends, and most importantly from the Father. He was honest and open. He prayed three prayers as he prepared for what lay ahead.

In his first prayer (Matthew 26: 39), He prayed, "My Father, if it be possible, let this cup pass from me: nevertheless not as I will, but as thou will." I believe Jesus was blatantly saying, "Father, if there is a way for me not to undergo this horrible ordeal of taking on the sins of the world and to be separated from you, then please spare me! Yet, not my will but your will be done."

Emptiness reveals our powerlessness

In his second prayer, there is a slight change in prayer, but a change nonetheless. In Matthew 26: 42 Jesus said. "My Father, if this cannot pass away unless I drink it, your will be done." By the time Jesus prayed this prayer there was less resistance. He had surrendered to drinking the cup, for He knew the Father's will. The Bible says He prayed again the same prayer. Sometimes one prayer is not enough. The important thing is to pray to the point of emptiness.

There are so many lessons to be learnt from Jesus about praying to the point of emptiness.

- Pray (share your heart) until you have emptied yourself. (Matthew 26: 39 and 42)
- Align your will with God's. (Matthew 26: 42)
- Receive the power to accomplish his will. (Matthew 26: 46)
- Arise and conquer. (Matthew 26: 46)

Prayer

Father, I pray that I may come to the end of myself and realise the power of being empty so that You can truly fill me. Father I pray that I may come to the realisation that I am dead to sin and truly alive in Christ. Therefore, Lord, I ask that You will rid me of all pride that stops me from realising my need for You. Lord, I pray that I will learn from the mistakes of the disciples, not to allow fear to cause paralysis in me, but to be quick to share my heart like Jesus did. May I realise that the answer is in You. Therefore, I will pray until I have the victory to conquer my fears and anxieties and to align my will with yours. May you, Lord Jesus, increase in me. I declare more of You and none of me. I choose to empty myself so You can fill me to capacity! In Jesus' name I pray. Amen!

Chapter 5

One Body, One Lord

The body is the church, the people. The body of Christ is comprised of all the believers who have accepted Jesus as Lord. We are part of a big family, and we all have the same blood of Jesus running through our veins. We are part of one body. That is, the body of Christ Himself. We are one, working towards a common goal—the will of God to be accomplished on earth.

In the same way, there is one God, yet He is three in one, with different functions and roles. God the Father's role and function is different to that of Jesus and that of the Holy Spirit, and yet they flow together as one. We all have different functions and roles in the body of Christ.

In John 17: 4 Jesus said, "I glorified thee on the earth having accomplished the work which you have given me to do."

Remember, as was established in Chapter 3, we are the followers. If Jesus had work to accomplish, so do we! Therefore we need to ask our Lord, to reveal to us what his purpose is for us individually. Each of us has a role, and unless we fulfil that role, we can never fulfil our God-given destiny, nor will we truly be fulfilled in God's kingdom. It is therefore crucial for us to know our role so we can live purposeful lives rather than be wanderers.

> *For in fact the body is not one member but many. If the foot should say, because I am not a hand, I am not of the body, is it therefore not of the body? And if the ear should say, "Because I am not an eye, I am not of the body," is it therefore not of the body? If the whole body were an eye, where would be the hearing? If the whole body were hearing, where would be the smelling? But now God has set the members each one of them, in the body just as He pleased, And if they were all one member, where would the body be? (1 Corinthians 12: 14-21)*

The above passage outlines the different parts of the body, illustrating some of the roles that we have. Some of us are the eyes; we can see past the natural into the supernatural and see into the very hearts of men. Some of us are the ears. Ever since I was a little girl, I noticed that I would hear someone say something, and I would most times hear or understand what was not said or hear the heart behind what was said. Some of us are the feet; we will go anywhere for Jesus, for a brother or sister to make sure they are okay.

However, whether you are an ear, brain, or even a toe, your functions are all important for the whole body to work as one. Doctors have claimed that without the smallest toe we would lose our balance and topple over. So, even if we are the smallest part of the body of Christ, our role is invaluable and is needed for the entire body to successfully work as one.

When I got the revelation that I had a role, I felt valuable. I then began to understand that I could not fulfil Mary's or John's role, only the role I was anointed for. I genuinely saw a change in myself because I felt accepted and significant for who I am, not for who I could be or who I wished I was. This revelation added so much value. I was no longer sitting in a service feeling jealous and competitive or leaving church feeling discouraged because I had compared myself to others so much that I felt as small as a peanut.

This comparison and competitiveness had so consumed me that when there was a visiting minister with prophetic gifting, I would be consumed with getting a prophetic word. I found it difficult to be happy for the prophetic word a sister or brother received. I could not even be in agreement in prayer if something was seen that we needed to wholeheartedly come against in prayer. I would never go to someone who had a profound prophetic word and say, "That was a great word you got. I am praying for you." No, the competitiveness in me would not allow me. You see, I lacked understanding of my value and acceptance in Christ. Also, my individual calling and destiny in the body of Christ had caused me to feel competitive and insecure. Could this be true for most of us?

When we have a revelation about our role, we will put to death those self-centred thoughts that cause us to make comparisons. We will stop being critical and competitive, ultimately causing division rather than cultivating oneness. I learnt a valuable lesson then. The kingdom of God is not about you and me being advanced. It is about the will of God being accomplished. We must then ensure not to

> *The kingdom of God is not about you and me being advanced. It is about the will of God being accomplished.*

interfere with God's divine will. These self-centred thoughts can cause us to fight against each other using slander, gossip, and negative confessions. If we are not building with God, we are fighting against Him.

When we come into agreement about our role, we will be secure in our relationship with Christ, understanding that we are completely accepted by our Father in heaven and that as children of God we are on the same side. Being on the same side means we are God's army. We all have different roles and functions, but as a team we are invincible like the people building the tower of Babel in Genesis. God Himself said about the people as they built the tower, "Nothing would be impossible for them" as they worked as one. It is crucial that we understand that individually we can only get this far and no further but that as an army equipped with our different gifts, roles, and functions, we will truly see the Church of Jesus Christ advanced and fulfil our God-given destiny.

This stresses how important it is to ". . . encourage each other daily and not to give up meeting together as some are in the habit of doing" (Hebrews 10: 24-25). When we work as a team we will be victorious. To stand as an army of the Living God is to declare war on the enemies of God. To endeavour to tackle the enemies of God alone is not only foolish but it is suicidal. When we embrace ourselves and our roles wholeheartedly, we are walking in oneness with God.

One People

In the book of Acts, before the baptism of the Spirit, the differences between races, classes, and religions still existed. In fact, this is why the Apostle Paul was divinely assigned to bring God's secret of salvation to the Gentiles. However, on the day of Pentecost (Acts 2: 8-11), God used Peter to draw many believers from different nations who spoke different languages than his own. It was always God's desire to gather different peoples with different languages as one. Yet, because they were all Jewish believers, it was still believed by others that salvation was only for the Jews.

Eventually God revealed to Peter what his plans were concerning his people. In Acts 10 Peter saw a vessel descending with all manner of unclean animals. The voice in the trance said to Peter, "Rise up, Peter, slay and eat!" Peter's response in verse 14 exposed his adherence to Jewish traditions: "By no means, Lord, for I have not eaten anything unholy and unclean." In this example in the Bible, God is showing us how he perceives people. He does not see people in groups, sects, colours, races, or classes, but as one and the same.

The apostle Paul, though he was a scholar in the Jewish religion, tells us in 1 Corinthians 12: 13 that we are all baptised into one body "whether we are Jews or Greeks". In Galatians 3: 27-28 Paul writes that for those who have put on Christ "there cannot be Jew and Greek." Also, in Colossians 3: 10-11 Paul tells us that we are a new creation with a brand new nature, it does not matter whether you are Jamaican, Indian, Polish, or American. Christ is all that matters, and He lives in all of us. Therefore, in Christ we are

Christians. This scripture illustrates the superb renewing of mind in Paul that we should endeavour to attain.

Humanly speaking, the differences between races cannot be overlooked; our environment and how we are nurtured influence our habits and our characters. In fact, these two factors—nature and nurture—have had such an impact on us that we must ask the Lord to give us His eyes to see people from His point of view. Not from our own worldly point of view.

Fundamentally, to align ourselves with God's vision for us is to be one; we cannot hold a worldly view of each other. Instead we must choose to see each of us as one in Christ. In Romans 6: 3-4 our baptism into Christ was a burial with Him into death. Therefore, our race, our rank in society, our background, and our colour were all buried with Christ, and thus we are walking in a new life.

In the book of Acts we can see numerous examples where the early church walked in oneness and the blessings they reaped as a result. They met in one place despite the fact that they were from different nations. The result was that power came down from heaven and miraculous signs and wonders were performed by the apostles. Believers were one in heart and mind, and what they owned was not their own. They shared everything they had (Acts 4: 32-35), and the result was that no one was in need.

For us to have these results we must:

- Know what our roles and functions are in the body of Christ. (1 Corinthians 12)

- Renew our minds about how we see different groups of people. (Colossians 3: 10-11)
- Put on love which binds us together as one. (Colossians 3: 14; 1 Corinthians 13: 1-4)
- Encourage each other in our roles and functions. (Hebrews 3: 13)

Prayer

Father, I thank You that You have a magnificent plan for our lives and that the good work You have begun in us, You will bring to completion. Father, I thank You that I don't have to compare myself to anyone because in your eyes I am special. Thank You that you sent your only Son to live, die and be resurrected so as to demonstrate your love for me. Father, I thank You that I am a part of a divine family where I am one with You. I thank You that You love me as much as You love Jesus. I thank You that when You look at me You see Jesus, not my race, colour, position, or class. May I adhere to Your vision and see segregation, cliques, prejudice, and discrimination come to an end among your children. I pray that collectively as a church we will encourage and build each other up to fulfil our functions and roles in your kingdom and thus as one unit see your kingdom advanced for your glory. I pray we will endeavour to know your will so that we can fight together towards your purpose rather than our own purposes. Father, I ask that You put to death in us all selfish ambition and self-promotion. Instead, I ask that You divinely connect us to those with whom we can be joined to as one and conquer and possess all that You have for us. Lord, I pray like Jesus, who accomplished the

Christine Nelson

work You gave Him to do. So it will be for us. Lord, I pray that You make clear what our role is so that we can live out Your dream and see our God-given destiny fulfilled. In Jesus' name, Amen.

Chapter 6

Flesh or the Spirit?

Romans 8: 4 says, *"That the righteousness of the law might be fulfilled in us, who walk not after the flesh but after the Spirit."* The word "walk" in Greek means to live and move.

2 Corinthians 3: 17 goes on to say that the Spirit is the Lord Himself. Therefore, to walk in the Spirit is to live and move in the Lord. That is, to walk in obedience to his will.

How we live greatly depends on the mind-set we have. If our mind-set is based on the world's view, then we walk in the flesh (Romans 8: 5). If our mind-set is based on the word of God then we will walk in the Spirit (Romans 8: 6).

After Saul had Stephen stoned to death in Acts 9: 3, Jesus appeared to Saul and asked him, "Why are you persecuting me?" In Saul's mind, he was doing the work of God by executing people whom he thought were blasphemers. Finally, a voice from heaven spoke to him and told him that he was persecuting Jesus. The message Jesus was trying to convey was that how we treat one another reflects how we treat Him, because we are a part of Him or one with Him by being united to Him through our faith. Therefore, how we treat our spouses, our children, or a stranger on the street is a reflection of our treatment of Jesus.

If this were our mind-set, it would certainly have a lasting effect on our actions, our reactions, the choices we make, and what we say.

I can remember when I was studying to become a teacher, all the different campus ministries in our church came together to produce a presentation. Each campus was to produce an act using singing, poetry, dance, etc. to present to Jesus as a gift. So these acts had to be excellent and presented from a pure heart! I remember having mixed feelings. I felt excited as well as some trepidation. I felt so privileged to be able to do something for Jesus—hence my excitement. The trepidation I felt was because I wanted desperately for it to be acceptable before Him, so I was determined to give my very best. The girls and I practised and practised to ensure that our performance was perfect.

Jesus is our only audience.

Soon the day came for us to perform a song from the movie *Sister Act 2*. When I am going to perform I am usually very nervous, because I am concerned about how well I will be received by the audience. Surprisingly, I wasn't nervous about the people. To my amazement (and to God be the glory) I did not consider them to be my audience, I simply remember just wanting to please Jesus. He was my only focus.

In our everyday lives, our focus needs to be on pleasing Jesus. The same respect and honour that we would give to Him, we should also afford to others. Walking in oneness with God means that we should also walk in love with one another. Our words, attitudes, and actions need to be aligned or in oneness with the Spirit of God.

In 1 Corinthians 2: 14 through 3: 3, Paul distinguishes between three kinds of people in relation to life in the Spirit: the natural person, the spiritual person, and fleshly person. However, in this chapter we will focus on the spiritual and the fleshly person.

Dr Neil T. Anderson in his book *Victory over the Darkness* describes the differences between the spiritual person and the fleshly person so distinctly.

The Spiritual Person

The spiritual person's spirit becomes united with God's Spirit at conversion. The soul of the spiritual man reflects a change caused by spiritual birth. His mind has been renewed and transformed. His emotions are characterized by peace and joy instead of turmoil. He is free to choose not to walk according to the flesh, because he is dead to sin. As the spiritual man exercises his choice to live in the spirit, his life exhibits the fruit of the spirit (Galatians 5: 22-23). The body of the spiritual person has been transformed. It is the dwelling place for the Holy Spirit and is being offered as a living sacrifice of worship and service to God. The flesh, which is conditioned to live independently from God under the old self, is still present, but he responsibly crucifies the flesh and its desires.

You might see this description and say, "Right! I am a Christian, and my behaviour, my thoughts, and my choices do not line up with this description." Though this is an ideal description, it is the model of maturity, toward which we are all growing, because we are a work in progress.

The Fleshly Person

The fleshly person is a Christian, spiritually alive in Christ and declared righteous by God. However, instead of being directed by the Spirit, this believing man chooses to follow the impulses of his flesh. As a result, his mind is occupied by carnal thoughts, and his emotions are plagued by negative feelings. Though he is free to choose to walk after the Spirit and produce the fruit of the Spirit, he continues to involve himself in sinful activity by wilfully walking after the flesh. The fleshly man's physical body is a temple of God, but it is being defiled. He is not presenting his body to God as a living sacrifice. He is yielding to the flesh instead of crucifying it. The fleshly man is also subject to feelings of inferiority, insecurity, inadequacy, guilt, worry, and doubt.

Spiritual Person	Fleshly Person
Crucifies the flesh. (Romans 8:8)	Yield to habitual patterns and lives independent of God.
Transformed mind. (*Romans 12:2*) Single-minded. (Philippians 4: 6-8)	Double-minded. (James 1: 7)
Fruit of the spirit. (Galatians 5:22)	Walks after the flesh. (Galatians 5: 19)
Peace. (Colossians 3: 15) Joy. (Philippians 4: 4)	Unstable emotions.
Salvation. (John 3: 3; 1 John 3: 9) Forgiveness. (Acts 2: 38; Hebrews 8: 12) Assurance. (Romans 8: 16) Security. (Ephesians 1: 13, 14) Acceptance. (1 John 3: 1) Worth. (Ephesians 2: 10)	Spirit is alive but quenched. (Romans 8: 9; 1 Thessalonians 5: 19)
Body is the temple of God. (1 Corinthians 6: 19, 20) Present as a living and holy sacrifice. (Romans 12: 1)	Body attacked by stress-related illnesses, such as heart palpitations.

One of the things I believe we must accept is the importance of believing that we are dead to sin.

> *For if we have become one with Him by the baptism into death, so that just as Christ was raised from the dead by the glorious power of the Father, so we too might habitually live and behave in newness of life. We know that our old (unrenewed) self was nailed to the cross with Him in order that (our) body which is the instrument of sin might be made ineffective and inactive for evil, that we might no longer be the slaves of sin. (Romans 6: 5-6, amplified)*

> *We must believe God's truth before it can be a reality.*

According to this scripture, when we gave ourselves to Christ by becoming one with Him, our old selves died. That is, the ability for sin to rule over our mortal bodies was rendered impotent. If we allow sin to rule over us, then we do so by choice. When we embrace the truth that we are dead to sin, we will choose to live holy lives because we will not willingly allow sin to reign in us. The truth is that we are dead to sin; the fact is that we must choose to believe this truth before it becomes a reality.

> *Even so, consider yourselves also dead to sin and your relation to it broken, but alive to God (living in unbroken fellowship with Him in Christ Jesus). (Romans 6: 11, amplified)*

Oneness or having an unbroken fellowship with Christ is maintained when we realise that we are alive to God, yielding to his ways.

One of the habits I have discovered in my mortal body that I have struggled with for as long as I can remember is impatience. The Word tells me that love is patient, and I desperately want to walk in love. I have noticed that I am particularly impatient and irritable with my eldest son, because he is so much like me. At least, this was my excuse for a long time until I faced the fact that I was impatient because I knew that I could get away with it, which is plainly disrespectful. When I behave impatiently, I feel frustrated and helpless, and it often makes me angry with myself. However, I have noticed that when I have my friends around, I am able to exercise patience with him. I discipline him if he is naughty when my friends are present, but I ensure that I remain composed and try my best to be patient.

In effect, what I am doing is choosing to do what is right in the sight of God. I am not prepared to disclose my bad behaviour because someone is watching. This tells me that I am not helpless to change when I am on my own. So, even without the watchful eyes of my friends, I can choose to be patient, kind, and loving. The point is that it is a matter of choice. I must therefore choose to live as someone who is alive in God and dead to sin. When we do this, we are crucifying the flesh and no longer allowing our bodies to control us. Instead we are presenting our bodies as instruments of righteousness so we can be controlled by the Spirit.

How do we live by the Spirit?

Christine Nelson

We must remember that:

- Our audience is Jesus. He sees and hears all things.
- We are dead to sin.
- We must surrender our bodies as instruments to God.
- We must yield to the leading of the Holy Spirit.

Prayer

Father in heaven, I thank You that You have created a whole new life through Jesus for me to live. Thank You that I am free to choose to walk by the truth of your Word rather than the lies of the world. Father, give me the conviction to lean and yield to Your Spirit, for I know all things are possible with You. Father, I desire to walk in the spirit, not in the flesh. Lord, may my mind, emotions, will, and body align with your Word. Lord, I thank You that I will never give up but will continue to realise that I am being transformed little by little. I thank You that I already have the victory to be the spiritual person You have called me to be. I continue to pray for the renewal of my mind that I may always remember who I am in Christ and live out what has already been paid and bought for me by the blood of Christ. I am dead to sin. Therefore, I choose to live as the spiritual person You have designed me to be, not in my might but through Christ who strengthens me. In Jesus' name, Amen.

44

Chapter 7

Abiding in Christ

What does "abide" mean? "Abide" means to dwell, to remain, or to continue. The opposite of abiding is to walk independently.

To abide in the Lord is to live according to the leading of the Lord. Spending time with God, praying unceasingly, and being thankful by living a life of praise are the key ingredients to abiding in Christ.

When we are abiding, we seek the Lord in all things. Prayer and then thanksgiving cause us to depend on the Lord. In fact, Jesus promises that if we abide in Him and his words, whatever we ask will be ours (John 15: 7).

In John 15: 1-8 Jesus uses a tree to symbolically describe what it means to abide. He explained that He is the vine of the tree, while His disciples are the branches. A tree would die without the vine, because the vine provides the tree with the necessary food and nutrients it needs. A branch is an offshoot of the tree, and it grows and bears fruit because of the oneness shared with the vine. If the branch is cut off, it is no longer gaining the nutritional value that the vine provides. Hence, it will wither slowly and die.

Jesus is our source. Without his provision we are incapable of growth, change, or development. However, when we are one with the vine, we will grow and change. It is inevitable because of the infusion of life from the vine. Clearly, we cannot change ourselves (Romans 6: 15), and yet many of us have tried tirelessly, independent of God, because we do not believe John 15: 5, which says, ". . . apart from me you can do nothing."

Notice that in this illustration, Jesus states He is the vine but He also mentions the Father's role as a gardener. The Father prunes or cuts off any branch that does not bear fruit. The Father will not force us to abide. He has given us the choice to abide; if we abide we will bear fruit, and then he prunes us to bear more fruit. If we choose not to abide, then he cuts us off and we are cast into the fire and burned (John 15: 6). Clearly, for us to abide we have to choose to be his divine offspring. We cannot abide unless we are grafted into the vine.

> *To be one with the vine is to grow and change.*

Spending Time with God

Practically, we abide in Christ when we spend time with Him. This is a habit we must form, because apart from Him we can do nothing. Mark 1: 35 tells us that after Jesus had a full day the day before, healing the sick and driving out evil spirits from crowds of people; *"Early the next morning while it was still dark, Jesus got up left the house and went to a quiet place where he prayed."* After twenty years of walking with God, this scripture still challenges me because I am not a morning person. Jesus undoubtedly had a conviction to spend time with God. He knew from where He got his power. Do you know from where you get your power? We are empowered in those times with God, if we are truly being honest and open to the Holy Spirit.

Unceasing Prayer

A few years ago, I was feeling like my spiritual growth had become stagnant. I sought from the Lord why this was so. The Lord showed me that I had become stagnant because I was no longer taking Him at His Word. I was reasoning what He was saying, which inevitably stole my faith. This led me to depend on myself. I then exchanged the truth of God's word for a lie by rationalising.

As a result, it stunted my growth and caused me to feel bound and depressed. The example He gave me then is in Romans 4: 17-23 when God told Abraham that he would have a son. The Bible says in verse 18 that "he hoped against hope." That is, though he knew that his wife's womb was dead and he himself may have not been functioning sexually (a fact) he chose to believe God (the truth). He could have reasoned by considering the facts about their lack of ability to conceive and become depressed. Instead, he chose to believe what God said. Romans 4: 19-21 says, "Abraham did not waver in unbelief because he was fully assured that what God had promised He was able to perform." As a result Abraham became the father of many nations.

I recognized that reasoning has the power to steal our destiny. Abraham fulfilled his destiny because he chose to believe the truth about God rather than being thwarted by facts. Today we have the same choice. We can choose to put every thought under the microscope of the word of God and choose to believe truth rather than a fact or a complete lie. We must remember that God's word is no respecter of persons or situations and will always accomplish what it was sent to do.

I made a covenant with the Holy Spirit some time ago to pray about any thought that came to my mind. This constant prayer has helped me to choose the truth of God's word and has kept me connected to God, allowing peace to reign in my heart. It took away the double-mindedness and created a single focus. I would no longer be disillusioned by my circumstances. This prevented feelings of depression and anxiety. Instead, I feel free to hear the voice of God and to be led by the Holy Spirit.

Thanksgiving

Thanksgiving is the overflow of your heart when you are spending time with God and are praying unceasingly. These principles prevent worrying or anxiety; we are continuously casting our cares onto God through prayer.

Also, there are times when we have given a situation to God, but Satan brings it back to our minds. It is imperative that we thank God that we have given Him that situation and remain assured it is in big, capable hands. Thank God for what He is doing and what He will do. By doing this, you are placing your trust in God and you are keeping a single-minded focus.

These three principles—spending time with God, unceasing prayer, and thanksgiving—are what I believe to be important keys to abiding in Christ.

How do we cut ourselves off from the vine?

- prayerless-ness
- lack of the word
- lack of openness with God and man
- guilt and shame and condemnation
- believing the lies of Satan
- pride (independence)

Peter was a person who provides a good example of being independent and leaning on his abilities. In Matthew 26: 33 Jesus foretold Peter about his denial. Peter was adamant that even if everyone else left Jesus, he would not. Peter was not lying. He genuinely believed that when tested he would be faithful. Clearly, Peter did not know himself well enough. Peter had tremendous self-confidence rather than a reliance on God to sustain him. Later, in Matthew 26: 69-75, Peter not only denied Jesus once, he denied Him three times. Undoubtedly, this demonstrates the importance of us having a conviction about abiding rather than being independent of God. Like Peter, we need to see the dangers of relying on ourselves, because it can cause us to not only deny Jesus but destroy our very lives.

In contrast, we see a distinct difference with Jesus' dependence on God. Jesus, the Son of God, throughout his ministry always made time to pray, to find a quiet place to meditate. He understood the concept of abiding. Therefore, He chose to rely solely on the Father. This really shows Jesus' humility and dependency on God and his willingness to yield to God's will. What about us? Jesus obeyed His own words when He said "apart from me you can do nothing" (John 15: 5).

How do we know if we are abiding in Christ?

- walking as Christ walked (1 John 2: 6)
- love for the brethren (1 John 2: 10 and 3: 14-15)
- God's word abiding within (1 John 2: 14)
- doing the will of God (1 John 2: 17)
- permission of individual (1 John 2: 24-25)
- continued anointing (1 John 2: 27)
- freedom from sin (1 John 3: 6)
- keeping commandments (John 3: 24; John 15: 10)
- indwelling Spirit (1 John 3: 24)
- bearing fruit (John 15: 4 and 7)

(Notes from Dake's Annotated Reference Bible)

Prayer

Father, I pray for the very heart of Jesus. I thank You for the humility that Jesus showed us by his constant dependence on You. Lord, may I be like the deer that pants for streams of water. Give me such a thirst and a hunger to spend time with You, so as to be one with You in thought, in word, and in deed. Teach me the notion of praying unceasingly, thus depending on You all the time. I pray that as I depend through prayer, I may see all that You do and express thanksgiving and praise You. I thank You that I can be effective in the battle of my mind by taking captive every thought and bringing it under the microscope of prayer. As I pray, teach me how to leave things in your hands as an act of surrender. Father, I thank You that as I do that, I will surely see the results just as Abraham did. Father, may I prove myself faithful to fulfil all the characteristics that come with abiding in You. In Jesus' name I pray. Amen.

Chapter 8

The Power of the Word

In Jesus' prayer in John 17: 19 He refers to his own sanctification: "I sanctify myself that they themselves also may be sanctified in truth." Jesus is the Word and the Word of God sanctifies us.

The Word is truth. When I was initially studying the Bible as a teenager to know more about Christ, I asked the woman who was studying with me, "How can I know undoubtedly that the Word is true or from the mouth of God?"

Her answer was so simple. She replied, "Anything that is true can be tested." What she said churned over in my mind for some time. I wondered how I could put the Word to the test. I soon realised that by practising the Word, I was testing the Word to see if its promises were true. I am very pleased to say that as a result my life has never been the same. I have found that by practising the Word, it has proven itself to be true.

Christine Nelson

How Does the Word Sanctify?

James 1: 21-25 says that the Word of God is like a mirror. The more we look in the mirror, the more we really get to know ourselves. The Word exposes the issues of our hearts and empowers us to change.

Yet though we look in a mirror daily, how many of us have measured our noses, or have checked the exact width of our lips? James 2: 25 states that *"a man who looks intently at the perfect law, the law of liberty, and abides by it, not having become a forgetful hearer but an effectual doer, this man will be blessed in what he does."* Clearly, looking in the Word of God is not sufficient. The important thing here is what we do with what we have seen in ourselves that doesn't align with his Word.

In 2 Corinthians 3: 18 the same principle has been aptly put:

> And all of us, as with unveiled face, (because we) continued to behold (in the Word of God) as in a mirror the glory of the Lord, are constantly being transfigured into His very own image in ever increasing splendour and from one degree of glory to another (for this comes) from the Lord (Who is) the Spirit.

As we behold the Word of God, we can choose what reflection we see. It is able to highlight the things in our lives that are not in accordance with God's will. Likewise, when we are walking in God's will, we are a reflection of his Word. Prayer is powerful, but it does not transform us into

Christ's image. Only when we put the Word into practise does transformation occur.

The Word Cuts!

In Hebrews 4: 12, the Word of God is described as being so precise that it divides the soul from the spirit. The soul, as we know, is made of the will, mind, and emotions. We are a spirit, and we live in a body. Most times we confuse the spirit and soul and think they are one and the same. This scripture clearly distinguishes between them. The Word of God is able to tell the difference between the two.

According to Hebrews 4: 12, when you spend a lot of time in the Word, the dividing of soul and spirit happens. You are then able to discern whether you are being led by the spirit or by the soul (flesh). I also believe that this separation brings an alignment with the will of God, and when you are not in his will, you know it. You are able to feel or sense that separation or that lack of oneness. This ability to discern comes with being sensitive to the Spirit of God.

> *Obedience to God's word brings oneness.*

I have experienced this numerous times. On one occasion I had a dream where I was teaching some of the pre-teen children at my church. In the dream I was shocked to see myself with this group of children, because although I had the desire to be involved in the children's ministry in the future, I had no desire to teach the pre-teens. I was thinking more of the teenagers. I had put the dream out of my mind because I was not interested in this age group.

Christine Nelson

Almost immediately, I started to pursue working with the teens and not the pre-teens as I had seen in my dream. I was welcomed into the teen ministry with open arms, but as I delved deeper I started to feel uncomfortable in my spirit. Later, one of the sisters that helped with the pre-teens came and asked me if I would consider the pre-teens. I told her I would pray about it and get back to her because I felt cautioned by my spirit as I remembered my dream.

When I prayed about it, the Lord revealed to me the real issues of my heart. It was not the age group that I was battling with, but my pride, I did not want to be led by a particular leader, and hence I was trying to avoid the pre-teen ministry. This revelation made my decision even harder. After much turmoil in my spirit, I decided to follow God's leading rather than my own ideas. I then obeyed and started to work with the pre-teens. As soon as I gave my consent, there was an alignment in my spirit and I felt such peace. You see my soul (emotions) was saying one thing, but my spirit was saying another. The minute I was able to discern where my spirit was leading me and that it was in agreement with the will of God, I could peacefully take the path of least resistance. You see, we often listen to our emotions (which aren't in tune with God), and they lead us to take a path which presents us with challenges. In Jeremiah 17: 9 the Bible talks about our emotions (heart) being deceitful above all things.

> Peace indicates the spirit is leading. Turmoil indicates the flesh is leading.

Clearly, obedience to God's Word (i.e., the voice of God), whether it is the logos Word, the rhema Word, the prophetic

56

Word, dreams from the Lord, visions or Word of knowledge, brings alignment or oneness with the Lord. However, if we don't know the Word and the character of the Lord, we won't be able to align ourselves with Him. As we align ourselves with His Word, we are partnering with Him. We become intimately acquainted with God's character by:

- reading the Word
- meditating on the Word
- praying the Word
- obeying the Word
- speaking the Word

This brings about the oneness Jesus prayed about.

Prayer

Father, I thank You for Your Word which brings light and revelation. I pray for the grace to align my will with Yours. May I walk in obedience to Your Word. May I have such a tender heart that will always respond to Your Word with diligence. Father, I pray for an insatiable appetite to eat at Your table. As I eat your Word, sanctify me, expose me, and renew my mind. Help me to be able to discern when I am being led by my soul rather than the spirit. I come against any hardness of heart to Your Word. I ask that You reveal to me by Your Holy Spirit any sin that has caused fallow ground in my heart. Father, I thank You that You are always speaking to me, and I pray that You will open my spiritual ears that I may hear and give me the grace to obey. In Jesus' mighty name, Amen.

Chapter 9

Expression of His Glory

Jesus' prayer in John 17 is a prayer for us to be intimate with Him. We must accept that we cannot be one unless we have an intimate relationship with Him. It is through our intimacy with Him that oneness is cultivated. Then we will become a true expression of his glory.

John 17: 23 says, "I in them, and you in me that they may be perfected in unity." Jesus was praying for intimacy. That we would have such a close relationship with Him that people would know who He really is. Romans 6: 10-11 describes this intimacy as an unbroken fellowship with God—that is, enjoying or benefiting from an unbroken connection or association with God. We should hold our relationship with the Father, Son, and Holy Spirit in high regard, ensuring that we do nothing to jeopardize it. That means taking captive every thought, word, and deed and making it obedient to Christ.

> *Intimacy is an unbroken fellowship with God*

I often wonder why Satan is so determined to destroy marriages. Genesis 2: 24 says, "For this reason a man shall leave his father and his mother and be joined to his wife, and they shall become one flesh." As a married woman I can testify that the adventure of becoming one with my spouse is a challenge but not impossible. It is submitting to one another daily. Satan fights marriages because he knows that if oneness is achieved, then he cannot get a foothold.

Jesus describes Himself as the bridegroom and his church as his bride. It is important not just to be acquainted with the bridegroom but to have intimate knowledge of who He is. Certainly, we would not marry someone we did not know.

Another great example of the intimacy God craves with us is seen in the book of Genesis. God created Adam and Eve and put them in the Garden of Eden so that He could have fellowship with them. God would walk and commune with them. It was a very special relationship. As you read this story, it is easy to see how much God loved his creations. Satan saw Adam and Eve walking in oneness with God, and he was jealous. So he used the one command God gave to Adam to separate Adam from God. It is this same unbroken fellowship that God had with Adam and Eve that He wants with us today.

If we want a deeper more intimate connection with God, we must learn to share our feelings honestly with Him. By doing this we will draw close to God, and He will draw close to us (James 4: 8).

Moses was honest with God about his fears over leading the Israelites out of Egypt and into the promised land. In Exodus 4: 10 Moses pleaded with the Lord, *"Master, please, I don't talk well. I have never been good with words, neither before nor after you spoke to me. I stutter and stammer."* (MSG)

In his honesty with God, Moses highlighted his unbelief in his own ability and his doubt about God's choice of him to lead the Israelites. Nevertheless, God gave Moses an assistant, his brother Aaron, and He assured him that His presence would be with them both during the journey ahead. Moses cultivated an open and honest relationship with God. This led to the intimacy that was needed for God's will to be accomplished for His people. In the Bible you will see that God can use anyone to achieve His will. He often uses those who know of their inadequacy so they see the need to cultivate a personal and intimate relationship with Him.

In our society today, we often fail to be genuine with one another, not because we are mean, but because we are afraid to give our honest opinion just in case people don't accept us or in case we offend. We craft chameleon-like personas that we think others want to see and will like, just so that we will be accepted. We lie and pretend, and after a while of playing this game of charades, we forget who we really are and lose touch with our true feelings.

I can relate to this. For a large part of my life I did not know my earthly father. For as long as I could remember until I became a Christian, I would lie to all my friends about my father. In fact, none of my friends at the time knew that I did not have a relationship with my father. I was afraid that I would not be accepted by them. I knew I was different, and I wanted to fit in, so instead I made up many lies to create the father of my dreams. These lies only made me hardened to the truth about myself and prevented me from facing the pain of rejection and the abandonment I felt. Inevitably, they caused me to lose touch with my heart and avoid my emotions.

When I became a Christian I had to train myself to explore what I was feeling and what my fears and anxieties were. I learnt how to express myself to God by writing my prayers out and going for prayer walks and dinner dates with God. As I learnt to share my emotions with God, it became easier to be truly open with people. More importantly, I became more intimate with my Father in heaven and was able to truly embrace his love and acceptance.

2 Peter 1: 3 emphasizes the blessings that come when we really have an intimate relationship with God. It reads, *"His divine power has granted to us everything pertaining to life and godliness, through the true knowledge of Him who called us by His own glory and excellence."*

According to 2 Peter 1: 3 intimate knowledge gives us:

- grace
- peace
- godly life
- fulfilment of the promises of God
- partaking in the divine nature of God
- escape from the corruption of this world

How Are We Carriers of His Glory?

In John 17: 10 Jesus prayed, ". . . I have been glorified in them" (NASB). In the NIV translation it says, "Glory has come to me through them."

God's glory is the revelation of his character and presence. Do our lives reflect the character and presence of Jesus? Christians are the closest resemblance to Jesus some people will ever see. This means that our lives must be a walking advertisement of the goodness and love of God. Every time we display his character, we are clothing ourselves with his presence and He is glorified. However, the opposite of glory is shame. So if we bring our own character into disrepute, we are also tarnishing God's character. My prayer is that our lives will be a living memorial to God, and may all we do bring glory to his name. Simply by association, as the Father is glorified, so too are we. As Jesus said in John 17: 22, "The glory which You have given Me I have given them, that they may be one, just as We are one."

> *May our lives be a living memorial to God.*

If you have been reading this book and you do not know Jesus as Lord, then my prayer is that having seen the heart of Jesus through this prayer in John 17, you will make the important decision to give your life to Jesus so that you can have an intimate walk with Him and that you will truly be a carrier of His glory and display it everywhere you go. If you are ready to make this step of faith, then pray this prayer and find a Bible-based church and become interwoven into the body of Christ.

Prayer

Father, I know that I have broken your laws and my sins have separated me from You. I am truly sorry, and now I want to turn away from my past sinful life toward You. Please forgive me and put me on the right path. I believe that Your Son Jesus Christ died for my sins, was resurrected from the dead, is alive, and hears my prayer. I invite Jesus to become the Lord of my life, to rule and reign in my heart from this day forward. Please send your Holy Spirit to help me to obey You and to do Your will for the rest of my life. Lord, I thank You that now I can know You intimately and display your glory wherever I go. In Jesus' name I pray. Amen.

Chapter 10

Dwell in the Secret Place

The Bible describes three tiers of being in fellowship with God—the Outer Court, the Holy Place, and the Holy of Holies. The Outer Court, I believe, is symbolic of those of us that live in the body. A parallel can be drawn between this and the Israelites living in Egypt. The Holy Place represents the soul, which is the wilderness where the Israelites wandered for forty years. The Holy of Holies represents the spirit, which is the promised land, the land of Canaan.

In order to find out how to dwell in the secret place we have to first know where we are currently living. Are we living in the body, the soul, or the spirit? To answer this, we must explore to know what each place is like.

The Outer Court, or the land of Egypt, is where we are slaves. We are enslaved to our flesh or to our carnal nature. We have to be whipped, told off, or threatened in order for us to do what we are commanded. We always need someone to tell us what to do or where to go. We are continuously trying to be good by doing good deeds, but we are never good enough. We feel frustrated and discouraged most of the time. We see God as a slave driver rather than a loving father. We feel His presence has departed from us, because our prayers go unanswered. The sense of abandonment causes us to believe he no longer loves or cares about us.

In the wilderness, or the soul, we are happy in the morning but by evening we are miserable. This is because the cares of this world dictate our mood. Our attitudes are poor, so we are easily offended, speak negatively, complain, and grumble. We harbour bitterness and lack of forgiveness. We continue to live in turmoil rather than in God's rest. We seem to be dealing with the same things over and over again because of our double-mindedness. Rather than growing, we have become stagnant. We encounter God, but as quickly as we receive a Word we forget it. Subconsciously we create a barrier between ourselves and God, and this barrier renders God impotent. He is unable to work on our behalf because of our lack of faith in his Word.

> *God desires that we live in the Holy of Holies.*

The land of Canaan, or the spirit, is where we all want to be. This was God's intention from the beginning—that we would live in the Holy of Holies. There we can commune with God, walking hand in hand, connecting heart to heart, as He once did with Adam and Eve. In Canaan the food is good. Our enemies are miniature, and we are the giants. Our brothers Joshua and Caleb told us this in Numbers 14: 7. We eat the best of the land; therefore we are very well nourished. All our needs are met. We may not have seen all the blessings in Deuteronomy 28: 1-14 come to pass, but we are secure that they have been established, and therefore we wait patiently for their manifestation. We live by faith and not by sight. We know what it means to live in the rest of Christ (Hebrews 4: 11). We are wise and discerning; we understand and know that the ability to discern the Spirit and engage with Christ is vital. We are certainly not perfect, but we have learnt the secret of surrendering to God so that Christ will be formed in us and live through us.

The interesting fact is, God desires for us to be in the Holy of Holies. All of God's people left Egypt and journeyed into the wilderness. Although they saw the glory of God and God's power, the Israelites were stuck in the wilderness (realm of the soul), because of the state of their hearts. The alarming fact is that it was only Joshua and Caleb out of that generation of Israelites who entered the promised land. We see this same issue with the Hebrew Christians who had become stuck in the realm of the soul and were in danger of reverting back to Judaism.

How Do We Enter the Holy of Holies?

1. Know the difference between the soul and the spirit. This occurs by the spending time in the Word (Hebrews 4: 12).
2. Put faith in the blood of the Lamb and its redeeming power (Hebrews 10: 19).
3. Our flesh must be broken so we can pass through the veil in order to enter the Holy of Holies. (Hebrews 10: 20). To pass through the veil is what the high priest had to do in order to go to the Holiest of All. Our flesh must be broken or crucified with Christ so that we can follow after the Spirit.

There is not a set way to walk in oneness with the Lord. If I were to say that there was, I would be trying to put God in a box and He is too *big* to be confined.

I remember the first time I read Psalm 91, I was sitting on a bus and I had only read the first three verses.

> *He who dwells in the secret place of the Most High will abide in the shadow of the Almighty. I will say to the Lord, "My refuge and my fortress, My God, in whom I trust! For it is He who delivers you from the snare of the trapper and from the deadly pestilence. (Psalm 91:1-3, NASB)*

I then noticed, it mentioned at least three consequences of living in the secret place.

1. We will live under the God's shadow.
2. God will be our safe haven.
3. God will deliver us from any trap.

In that moment, I was desperate to know where this place was. I later came to realise it was a place of serenity, rest, meditation, revelation, unbroken fellowship with the Lord, unceasing prayer, and a heart-to-heart connection. My only way to describe this place is that it is within us. When you are there, your spiritual senses are heightened and you can have conversations with God as Moses had with Him. You can hear the Lord clearly. As you obey his voice, it becomes easier and easier to live in this *oneness* on a daily basis.

When I am not connected with the Lord in this way, I become irritable and cloudy in my thinking. When I become like this, I know it is time for me to physically go to my secret place to speak to the Lord, and like Jesus in the Garden of Gethsemane, I do not leave until I have completely poured out my soul. I have found doing this clarifies my own thoughts and cleanses me, leaving me feeling renewed.

In Psalm 63:1-2, David writes:

"O God Thou art my God,
I shall seek thee earnestly.
My soul thirst for Thee,
My flesh yearns for Thee,
In a dry and weary land where there is no water.
So I looked for you in the sanctuary, to see
Your power and Your glory"

So where are you?

> *Are you longing, thirsting or seeking God?*

When I am in the secret place, I get a glimpse of God's glory (his character and presence). It creates in me a longing, a hunger, and a thirst for more of Him. In his book *The Annointing*, Benny Hinn suggests that longing takes you to the Outer Court; thirsting takes you to the Holy Place; and seeking leads you to the Holy of Holies. The question is, are you longing, thirsting, or seeking God? When you can make sense of where you are at, then you will know if you are in the Outer Court, the Holy Place or the Holy of Holies.

The Journey

In the Holy of Holies, I don't have to say anything. In Psalms 46: 10 David wrote, "Be still and know that I am God." In fact, I do a lot of writing. If I am prompted to talk, I have some of the most amazing question-and-answer sessions with God. I then meditate and gain fresh revelations. This is where praying unceasingly becomes second nature. I am now having a complete three-course meal with trimmings from the very throne of God.

Have a Drink!

> *The living water of the Holy Spirit is the fuel needed for us to be sustained, so we can walk in oneness.*

Another important aspect of walking in oneness with God is always drinking from His Spirit. The latter part of 1 Corinthians 12: 13 says, "And we were all given to drink one spirit."

As we go through life, we can become drained, tired, and weary. In nature, when we become thirsty we become weak if we do not have a drink. Likewise, spiritual thirstiness leads to spiritual weakness. When we become dry we need to drink from the Holy Spirit. We should not wait until we become dry, but we should be able to discern or gauge where we are in the spirit. In John 4:14 Jesus told the Samaritan woman, "But whoever drinks of the water that I will give him shall never thirst; but the water that I will give him shall become in him a well of water springing up to eternal life."

I believe Jesus was referring to drinking from the Holy Spirit. The scripture teaches in 1 Corinthians 15: 45 that Jesus is the life-giving Spirit. So to drink of the Spirit is to be filled with Christ's life. With this comes empowerment to do the impossible. On our own we can do nothing, but with the Spirit of God all things are possible. In the secret place, we need to continuously ask for the drink Jesus offered the Samaritan woman. A fresh infilling of the Holy Spirit is the fuel needed for us to be sustained so we can walk in oneness.

Clothe Yourself

The unity of our human spirit and the Holy Spirit is where oneness begins.

The Spirit is life within us, but it also represents clothing for the physical body, symbolising authority and power. An example of this is seen in Acts 2: 1-4 when the early Christians were clothed with power. It is crucial that we too are clothed with God's power and live as overcomers.

Destination

To walk in oneness with God is to live in the Holy of Holies. The unity of our human spirit and the Holy Spirit is where oneness begins. It is in the Spirit that we become who we are in Christ, a new creation. It becomes easier to follow the example of Jesus, to imitate Christ, to empty ourselves, and to embrace the acceptance that comes with being a part of one body and one Lord and with walking in the spirit, not the flesh, truly making Christ our dwelling place and making the word of God the final authority over our lives. As we live this, we carry the very glory of Jesus everywhere we go, and we fulfil Jesus' prayer in John 17. We are Jesus' representatives here on earth, and as such our living in oneness with God will show unbelievers His true face and heart towards them. That will be on display, through our very lives.

How Do We Dwell in the Secret Place?

Moses said in Psalm 90: 1, "*Lord you are my dwelling place.*" He is our land of Canaan. We dwell in the secret place by living in Christ. Colossians 2: 6 says, "J*ust as you received Christ as Lord, continue to live in Him.*" To live in Him is to follow his lead by perceiving his will. Be "*rooted and be built up in Him" (Colossians 2: 7).* To be rooted in Him is to spontaneously live out Christ as He dwells within us in oneness so that everything we do and say is from Christ. As we do this, Christ is being formed in us more and more (Galatians 4: 19). The fact is that Christ is our everything. He is our food, our rest, our protection, and our light. We need to rely on Him for everything, knowing we cannot walk in oneness in our own strength. Recognizing our powerlessness, we are then empowered to live out the life of Christ.

> We dwell in the secret place by living in Christ.

To Maintain Oneness

- Ask the Lord to show you where the secret place is.
- Include Christ in all you do.
- Seek, long, thirst, hunger to be one with God.
- Surrender to the life-giving Spirit of Jesus and let Him live through you.

Prayer

Lord Jesus, since You are the Spirit that lives in me, I surrender myself and my all to You. I surrender my intellect, abilities, talents, ways, practises, mind, emotions, and will. Lord Jesus, it is no longer I that live but You who live in me. I want my actions and words to be firmly rooted in Your will. Teach me how to live in the spirit every minute of every day so I can continue to be one with You. Give me the ability to know where I am so that by Your grace I may live in the Holy of Holies and settle for nothing less. Lord, teach me how to include you in everything I do—in my marriage, nurturing my children, work, studies, and cleaning. I receive grace to drink from your Spirit and to draw from you all I need. May I always have the power to walk in oneness with you now and for evermore. Amen.

Biblical References on Oneness

This is a compilation of some basic scriptures that will assist in further study. The table below is an outline of the types of behaviour that can produce oneness and the behaviours that can destroy oneness.

Keys to Oneness	Enemies of Oneness
obedience	disobedience
prayer	prayerlessness
study and application of the Word	not immersing self in the Word
intimacy with Christ	acquaintance with God
the Word of God	slander/gossip
acceptance	rejection
evaluate	criticize
relationships	isolation
dependence on God	independence from God

> *God is a Spirit (a spiritual being) and those who worship Him must worship Him in spirit and truth. (John 4: 24, AMP)*

> *The last Adam (Jesus Christ) became a life giving Spirit (restoring the dead to life). (1 Corinthians 15: 45b, AMP)*

The Spirit within us is Jesus. He is a life giving Spirit.

> *Now the Lord is that Spirit and where the Spirit of the Lord is there is liberty. (2 Corinthians 3: 17, AMP)*

The Holy Spirit is within us and He brings freedom.

All three persons of the trinity (triune God) live within us as one

> *The Spirit Himself (thus) testifies together with our own spirit (assuring us) that we are children of God. (Romans 8: 16)*

The unity of the Spirit and our spirit that guarantee us children of God. With this agreement comes oneness.

> *The Lord Jesus Christ be with your spirit (2 Timothy 4: 22, AMP).*

The importance of Jesus being with my spirit is crucial for oneness to become a reality.

> *But I urge and entreat you, brethren, by the name of our Lord Jesus Christ, that all of you be in perfect harmony*

*and full agreement in what you say, and that you be
perfectly united in your common understanding and in
your opinions and judgements. For it has been made
clear to me, my brethren, by those in Chloe's household,
that there are contentions and wrangling and factions
among you. What I mean is this that each one of you
(either) says, I belong to Paul, or I belong to Apollos, or I
belong to Cephas (Peter) or I belong to Christ. Is Christ
(the Messiah) divided into parts? Was Paul crucified on
behalf of you? Or were you baptised into the name of
Paul. (1 Corinthians 1: 10-13a, AMP)*

Where there is division, it suggests a lack of renewal of the
mind and revelation of our oneness in Christ.

*Yes everything else is worthless when compared with
the priceless gain of knowing Christ Jesus my Lord. I
have discarded everything else, counting it all garbage,
so that I may have Christ and become one with him.
(Philippians 3: 8-9, NLT)*

Being One with Christ needs to be our ultimate goal.

*That together you may (unanimously) with united
hearts with one voice, praise and glorify the God and
Father of our Lord Jesus Christ (the Messiah). (Romans
15: 5-6, AMP)*

There is power in the unity of voice and praise of JESUS!!

*May He grant you out of the rich treasury of His glory
to be strengthened and reinforced with mighty power in
the inner man by the Holy Spirit (Himself) indwelling*

your innermost being and personality. May Christ through faith actually dwell (settle down, abide make His permanent home in your hearts! May you be rooted deep in love and founded securely on love. That you may really come to know practically through experience for yourselves the love of Christ, which far surpasses mere knowledge without experience that you may be filled through all your being unto all the fullness of God may have the riches measure of the divine Presence, and become a body wholly filled and flooded with God Himself. (Ephesians 3: 16-17a, 19b)

And put on the new nature (the regenerate self) created in God's image, Godlike in true righteousness and holiness. (Ephesians 4: 24)

And have clothed yourself with the new (spiritual self) which is (ever in the process of being) renewed and remoulded into fuller and more perfect knowledge upon knowledge after the image (the likeness of Him who created it. (Colossians 3: 10-11)

My little children, for whom I am again suffering birth pangs until Christ is completely and permanently formed (moulded) within you. (Galatians 4: 19)

The process of glorification where Christ takes over and we allow Him to live through us is key to oneness.

The spirit of man can know what the soul cannot. (1 Corinthians 2: 11)

Our spirit can discern what the soul cannot discern.

The Spirit bears witness with our spirit. (Romans 8: 16)

"But he who is joined to the Lord is one spirit." (1 Corinthians 6: 17)

This fellowship of both our spirit and the Spirit of God is what creates oneness.

Worship God in spirit and truth. (John 4: 24)

God can only be worshipped in the Spirit, emphasizing the need to dwell in the Spirit or the Holy of Holies.

When Christ, who is our life, appears, then you will appear with Him in glory. (Colossians 3: 4)

Christ is our life . . .

We always carry around in our body the death of Jesus, so that the life of Jesus may also be revealed in our body. For we who are alive are always being given over to death for Jesus' sake, so that his life may be revealed in our mortal body. So then, death is at work in us but life is at work in us too. (2 Corinthians 4: 10-12)

Dying to ourselves daily magnifies the wonder of living the resurrected life.

For in Him we move and have our being. (Acts 17: 28)

To move in Christ, not in ourselves.

Notes

Chapter 2: Jesus Our Example

The New American Standard Bible Key Word Study Bible Hebrew Greek, AMG publishers

Chapter 3: Followers that Follow

Finis Jennings Dake, Notes from *The Dake Annotated Reference Bible,* (1996)

Chapter 4: Emptying Yourself

The New American Standard Bible Key Word Study Bible Hebrew Greek, AMG publishers

Chapter 5: One Body, One Lord

http://www.livingstreamministry.com

Document title *Oneness in the Mingled Spirit* by Witness Lee (accessed May 9, 2010)

Chapter 6: Flesh or the Spirit

Dr Neil T Anderson, *Victory over the Dark-ness,* (1992) Monarch Books

Chapter 7: Abiding in Christ

Finis Jennings Dake, Notes from *The Dake Annotated Reference Bible,* (1996)

Chapter 10: Dwell in the Secret Place

Benny Hinn, *The Annointing*, (1992) Thomas Nelson Publishers.

Witness Lee, *The Economy of God*, (1968) Living Stream Ministry